AFFIRMING CATHOLICISM

Stephen Cottrell

CATHOLIC
EVANGELISM

Series Editor: Jeffrey John

D1248070

DARTON · LONGMAN + TODD

First published in 1998 by
Darton, Longman and Todd Ltd
1 Spencer Court
140–142 Wandsworth High Street
London SW18 4JJ

in association with

Affirming Catholicism
St Giles Church
No 4, The Postern
Wood Street, The Barbican
London EC2Y 8BJ

ISBN 0–232–52271–5

The views expressed in this booklet are those of the
author and do not necessarily reflect any policy
of Affirming Catholicism

Designed by Bet Ayer
Phototypeset by Intype London Ltd
Printed and bound in Great Britain by
Page Bros, Norwich

Affirming Catholicism

Affirming Catholicism is a movement (not an ecclesiastical party) which exists to do two things. We affirm our confidence in our Anglican heritage; and we seek to renew and promote the Catholic tradition within it. Our aim is to explore, explain and share with others both inside and outside the Church a lively, intelligent and inclusive Catholic faith. In the words of our Trust Deed:

> It is the conviction of many that a respect for scholarship and free enquiry has been characteristic of the Church of England and of the Churches of the wider Anglican Communion from earliest times, and is fully consistent with the status of those Churches as part of the Holy Catholic Church. It is desired to establish a charitable educational foundation which will be true both to those characteristics and to the Catholic tradition within Anglicanism ... The object of the foundation shall be the advancement of education in the doctrines and the historical development of the Church of England and the Churches of the wider Anglican Communion, as held by those standing within the Catholic tradition.

Our Publications

These are offered as one means of presenting Anglican Catholic teaching and practice in as clear and accessible a form as possible. Some cover traditional doctrinal and liturgical themes; others attempt to present a well-argued Catholic viewpoint on issues of debate currently facing the Church. There is a list of our series of booklets on page v.

The present series of books is provided, where appropriate, with summaries to sections, and suggested questions which we hope will facilitate personal study or discussion in groups. Other titles in the series are:

Christian Feminism – an Introduction Helen Stanton
Humanity and Healing – Ministering to the Sick in the Catholic Tradition Martin Dudley

To order these publications individually or on subscription, or for further information about the aims and activities of Affirming Catholicism, write to:

The Secretary
Affirming Catholicism
St Giles Church
No 4, The Postern
Wood Street
The Barbican
London EC2Y 8BJ

Tel 0171 638 1980
Fax 0171 638 1997

Books in the Affirming Catholicism series

About the Author

Stephen Cottrell is a Missioner with Springboard, the initiative of the Archbishops of Canterbury and York for Evangelism. He is also Diocesan Missioner and Bishop's Chaplain for Evangelism in the missionary Diocese of Wakefield.

He is one of the authors of *Emmaus, the Way of Faith*.

Contents

The Christian community is never closed in upon itself. The intimate life of this community – the life of listening to the Word and the Apostles' teaching, charity lived in a fraternal way, the sharing of bread – only acquires its full meaning when it becomes witness, when it evokes admiration and conversion, and when it becomes the preaching and proclamation of the Good News. Thus it is the whole Church that receives the mission to evangelise.

Evangelii Nuntiandi

'I am the vine, you are the branches. Whoever remains in me, with me in him, bears fruit in plenty.'

John 15:5

Introduction

What is evangelism?

First of all, what do we mean by evangelism? Sometimes it is confused with mission.

Mission refers to 'everything that the Gospel of God's love revealed in Christ sends to the world. It embraces the pursuit of justice and peace and the care of creation, as well as the sharing of faith.'[1] Evangelism is therefore that aspect of mission which is concerned with bringing people to faith in Christ. It cannot be separated from the whole of God's mission, but for the purposes of this book will be dealt with on its own in a sharp focus.

And what about evangelisation? This is the term preferred by the Roman Catholic Church. Actually the terms are almost interchangeable. Evangelism tends to stress the proclamation of the gospel; evangelisation tends to stress the whole process of coming to a commitment to Christ and his Church. Thus, as Christians, we are able to say that we have made a commitment to Christ but are not yet fully evangelised.

It has been said that evangelisation is also about the influencing of cultures as well as individuals. But this sounds to me like mission. So in this book we will stick to the two simple terms: mission – meaning our sharing in everything that God has done, and is doing, for us in Christ; evangelism – meaning that part of mission by which people become disciples of Jesus Christ.

What is Catholic evangelism?

In one sense that is what this book sets out to discover. Is there anything distinctive about Catholic evangelism as compared with the evangelism of any other tradition of the Christian Church? The fact that Roman Catholics tend to prefer the word evangelisation gives us our first clue. As I have said, this word suggests a process. Although for the rest of this book I am sticking to the word evangelism – chiefly because I prefer to keep the cutting edge this word possesses – I will be describing a process. Catholic evangelism is about the journey of faith. It begins when a community of believers understands its vocation as sharing in God's mission of love to the world. Catholic evangelism is about becoming a missionary and evangelistic church. Its first fruit is renewed service to the local community. Catholic evangelism is shaped by Catholic spirituality. It is about the incarnation – finding God in human life – and it is about service. Its method is that of the accompanied journey. We learn how to share faith with people, challenge people to respond to the call of the gospel and accompany them on a journey that leads to commitment and church membership. Catholic evangelism will be rooted in the ideas of the catechumenate. It will also be about bringing people to the life of the church, as well as to personal commitment to Jesus. It will help people grow to maturity of faith and active discipleship. The aim of Catholic evangelism is that all baptised Christians should share an apostolic ministry.

Isn't all ministry evangelistic?
My definition of mission is very broad. So, yes, all ministry seeks to take its agenda from God's mission of love to the world. But evangelism is distinctive. It provides the cutting edge to mission. Without a specifically evangelistic ministry our mission ceases to be specifically Christian. There are all sorts of people who are concerned with justice and peace and building what we would call the Kingdom of God. This is very good. We rejoice in the witness and example of all people of goodwill and of whatever faith. We are happy to work with them wherever our agendas coincide. But the Christian gospel demands that we care for the whole person. Therefore our ministry must address spiritual as well as physical need. We are concerned for the human heart as well as the stomach and the mind. The gospel we share is a joyful declaration of abundant life. 'I have come that you may have life in all its fullness', says Jesus.[2]

The theological rationale for this evangelism is plain and simple: Jesus' great commission at the end of Matthew's Gospel.[3] But Jesus does not say 'go and make converts', he says 'go and make disciples'. This is a process which begins by hearing of God's great love for us in Christ and proceeds by way of repentance and faith to a new and abundant life. Having realised we are on a journey home, we live our lives as citizens of heaven. Our whole lives are focused on God. This is the real meaning of the biblical word repentance. Not just saying sorry, but a complete turning around: a reorientation of our life.

This is what evangelism is concerned with: making disciples. The distinctive contribution that Catholic Christians can make is to see this as a process which involves the whole church and leads people to active discipleship within the church. This book attempts to explain how this process can take place, and how it can and should be the central concern and raison d'être of the church. Part 1 of the book is more theoretical, looking at how to get evangelism at the heart of the agenda of a missionary church. Part 2 is more practical, looking at how we develop the structures and ministries in the church so as to see people come to faith. But running throughout the book is a Catholic theology of mission and practical steps towards putting all of this into practice. It is written especially for Catholic Christians, who sometimes think that evangelism is not for them, but also for all Christian people since we all belong to the one, holy, catholic and apostolic Church. It is published under an Affirming Catholicism heading but is for all Christians and certainly for all catholics – Roman Catholics and Anglican Catholics of both integrities. This is one area where we can all be united. Indeed, Jesus prayed that we may be one in order that the world may believe.[4]

PART ONE

GETTING EVANGELISM ON TO THE AGENDA

Becoming a Missionary Church

***

A changing culture

We are now coming towards the close of the Decade of Evangelism. Not many people seem to speak about the Decade any more. Is this because we now consider the whole thing to have been an embarrassing mistake? After all, the statistics about church attendance give us little comfort. Or is it because the Decade of Evangelism has actually succeeded in what was one of its most important aims: getting evangelism onto the agenda of the local church? The very fact that I have been asked to write this book is evidence of a growing awareness that the Church needs to learn how to share its faith with others. For centuries we lived in a comparatively stable society where the model for being the church was based around an understanding of our culture and society as being basically Christian. Our job, as the church, was to teach people the faith and care for them. We understood our role in a predominantly pastoral way.

All this is rapidly changing. There is very little sense in now calling Britain a Christian country. This is not just a matter of Sunday trading laws – though it is remarkable how the nature of Sunday has been transformed in a matter of years – it is about the whole way we feel about ourselves, and the very different ways we choose to gain identity and purpose for life. Even thirty years ago, when I started junior school, though I was not part of a churchgoing family, I was brought up with some awareness that I was part of a Christian country and shared in a commonly owned set of beliefs and values. This is not the same today. The very fact that we describe our society as *post*-modern says more about what we are leaving behind than what we are entering into. We live in a questioning society that is highly suspicious of the big, all-embracing answers of the past. For many people, therefore, Christianity takes its place on the back burner of history, along with many of the other ideologies that played such a large part in shaping the life and aspirations of this century.

Into this vacuum has come a whole variety of other ways of making sense of life. Be it a high fibre diet and plenty of exercise, Zen Buddhism or psycho-analysis, there is plenty of evidence to show that people still thirst for meaning in their lives. What has changed is that there is no one all-embracing spiritual, psychological, or for that matter political or economic philosophy which a majority of people look to. The society in which we live is both pluralist and relativist. I do not mean this in any pejorative sense. This is just a description of the way we are: there are many truths to look to, and what is true for me may not be true for you. As Louis MacNeice observed, 'the world is crazier and more of it than we think. Incorrigibly plural'.[5] It is unlikely that this poem could have been written before the Somme, Auschwitz and finally Hiroshima blew away the optimistic certainties of the Enlightenment.

This is the world the church finds itself in. A common image for it is the supermarket (after all, shopping seems to be the great pastime of the post-modern world). There are many ways to find meaning in life and they are all laid out on the supermarket shelves; but, and here is the rub, no one thing has any greater claim to truth than another. In fact all are welcome to display their wares so long as they do not oppress the rival claims of others by declaring a universal truth. In fact it is this claiming of universality which is the very thing our age is recoiling from. 'Post-modern' and 'post-enlightenment' are better described as 'post-ideological'. Christianity is seen as one ideology among many. It is fine for you to believe those things provided you do not claim that the ideas that help you find purpose in your life have an equal claim on mine.

Even this very brief look at the kind of culture in which we are called to evangelise shows with harsh clarity the main problems facing the Church. We believe the gospel of Jesus Christ is the saving truth for all people of all ages, yet we are living in an age which is increasingly suspicious of anybody who makes universal claims for anything. Here I am not just talking about religious claims: there is a growing relativism towards all commonly held beliefs about the world, and this affects science, religion, literature and all schools of human thought. The reaction against the optimism of the Enlightenment is an attack on rationalism of any kind. This is truly the 'new age' we hear so much about.

Little wonder that all the major Christian Churches called for a decade of evangelism! Little wonder that we are finding things so hard. Even without the changing culture which gives a wide berth to the universal claims of Christian faith, busy clergy and committed Christian people are being asked to change the way they think about the church. No longer is church just about caring for people and teaching them the faith – the pastoral model I alluded to above. We have now tagged on the task of finding people in the first place!

A responsive church

There is no need to despair. It is the first time for a long time that we have been in a situation like this, but it is *not* the very first time. Our multi-faith pluralist society has some interesting similarities with the world of the Roman Empire into which the Christian faith was born. Then the Christian faith had to jostle and harry alongside many other philosophies and religions. In the end it won the day for three distinctive reasons:

1. the credibility and intellectual integrity of the faith that was being shared;
2. the ability of faith to clothe itself in the various cultures it encountered;
3. the evidence in people's lives for the veracity and transforming energy of the gospel.

In other words the work of evangelism (the making known of the gospel of Jesus Christ) was woven tightly together with apologetics (the reasoning, arguing and commending of faith) and spirituality (the lived experience of Christian life).

These are issues we will return to, but the point I want to make here is that evangelism was effective because it was bound up with being a church in mission. It was conscious of its great commission, but untarnished by either the triumphalism that would seek to ride roughshod over other strongly held beliefs, or the complacency which merely waits for people to come to you. In those first centuries the church had either to be a missionary church or not a church at all.

Pastoral evangelism

It is not that in today's situation the pastoral ministry of caring for people and teaching them the faith is unimportant, but that it is necessary to locate this ministry within the missionary dynamic. As we rediscover how to do evangelism, we must also relearn apologetics and re-energise our spirituality. This will mean more pastoral care, not less. In this respect some of the slogans which heralded the beginning of the Decade of Evangelism have served us poorly. We were told that we should move from maintenance to mission and from pastoral care to evangelism. But these are false distinctions. We cannot simply stop maintaining the church as we have inherited it from the past; neither can, or should, we stop caring for each other. Not only is the quality of our caring relationships one of the biggest magnets to the Christian life, but ask any priest and he will tell you that the first fruit of evangelism is more pastoral care!

With regard to maintenance I want to argue that

we should fight our battle on two fronts. On the one hand we need to maintain the church as we have inherited it, and at the same time we need to be planting and nurturing the church of the future. With regard to pastoral care I want to argue that our problem is that we have not been pastoral enough! We have either seen pastoral care as entirely separate from evangelism, or, even where there is a connection, allowed pastoral care to become something much less than the nurture of a Christian community which is its main purpose. It has become highly individualised: one individual – usually the priest – looking after all the other individuals. It has not been *one another care* within the body of the church, neither has it been about body building: growing a Christian community in faith and love, the real business of being a caring church.

Being a priest today is a tough job. But our models for ministry need to reflect the reality of God who is Father Son and Holy Spirit.[6] We need a much more collaborative pattern of ministry, with the priest as the animator of the Body so that the pastoral and evangelistic ministries become part of the one ministry of the one church. The missionary church is also the pastoral church.

Saving truth

The Church of the first few centuries displayed an astonishing commitment to the truth of the gospel. Many people died rather than deny that truth. It would have seemed like fanaticism were it not for the gracious humility with which people turned the other cheek and offered forgiveness to those who persecuted them. We need that kind of commitment. Unless we are a church which is committed to the truth, then, to put it crudely, there will be no one to teach and no one to care for and no church at all. We must believe that our faith, without standing in unnecessary judgement on other beliefs and ideas, holds life and death truth for every human being. We must be prepared to live by this truth and share it with others. It is wise to remember that the church is always only one generation away from extinction.

What is needed is a change of mindset. We no longer live in Christendom. We are not the only item on the supermarket shelf. It is not self-evidently the case that we are the best item on offer. Certainly, we are not the most attractive. Our faith makes huge claims about itself and massive demands on those who follow in its way. Therefore this is one book about evangelism which will not argue that what is required is simply a jazzy repackaging to solve all our ills or, worse, a redesign of the product itself. A theme running through this book is the *spirituality* of evangelism. We follow a crucified Lord: Jesus by all present-day standards of church growth and evangelism was something of a failure. By arguing that we become a missionary church I am not exhorting us to become a 'successful' church. That way of thinking is part of our misunderstanding of evangelism, even if it is often fed by the hard-sell evangelism of well-intentioned, but over-zealous Christians. We need humility in our evangelism. We are stewards of the gospel for this generation. We need to teach the faith; we need to care for one another within the body of the church; and we also need to share the faith. This is the simple truth of what it means to be a *holy, catholic and apostolic church.*

To be a holy church means to be a church which is *in communion with God.* To be a catholic church means to be a church which is *in community with one another.* To be an apostolic church means to be a church which is *in communication with the world.*

This is the missionary mindset, and it is nothing more than being the church as God has always intended us to be. These are our priorities, always remembering that the primary call of the church is worship, not evangelism. But worship, properly understood, is not a private affair. It overflows with love and service to the world.

I have argued this in my Grove booklet, *Sacrament, Wholeness and Evangelism*: what we *do* as a church ought to arise out of an understanding of what God has called us to *be.* We need a new evangelism, but it must arise out of the call to be the missionary church in the world. What follows is a practical suggestion about how a church might rediscover its missionary calling by producing a simple mission statement and auditing its response to the call to be holy, catholic and apostolic.

We shall then turn to the ministry of evangelism itself. Here the catholic concepts of faith as journey and a deep-rooted mystical spirituality provide the keys to the new and holistic evangelism I am seeking to promote.

Step 1 – Producing a mission statement
A mission statement is a statement of purpose: it is a vision of what it means to be the church.

Many churches are bad at planning. Often this is because there is no agreed understanding of aims. A mission statement is a tool to help establish these aims.

Many churches imagine the choice facing them is between 'changing' or 'staying the same'. This is not so. One thing is certain: things will change. The real choice is between shaping the change oneself or being shaped by it. A mission statement is therefore an aid to creative decision-making and management of change. By agreeing on our purpose there is a yard-stick by which everything else can be measured, both the external changes in society which we have to respond to, and the internal changes whereby we try to shape our life around the call to be a holy, catholic and apostolic church.

Producing a mission statement need not be a diffi-cult or lengthy process. It is important that as many members of the church as possible are involved in the initial process, since it is a commonly owned vision for the church which will best enable it to be effective in its management of change and its planning for the future. At the very least the church council needs to be involved at every stage.

Here is a simple four-point plan for producing a mission statement. It is the first step towards becoming a missionary church.

1. Ask everyone to finish the following sentence as a way of expressing what the church is for.

   'The reason we have a church in N__ is ...'

   This could be done at the beginning or end of

Sunday worship, at an annual church meeting, or at a specially convened meeting, but is best when as many members of the church as possible can participate. It only takes five minutes. What you are after is a simple statement of purpose. A simple way of helping people into the exercise is to ask what sort of church they think Jesus wants them to be.

You now have a collection of mission statements.

2. Empower a small group of people to take away the statements and analyse their contents listing the different things mentioned and calculating what things are mentioned the most.

   This process is much simpler than it sounds. On the whole this process is not about breaking new ground but reminding ourselves of what we have always known but rarely call to mind. You will be surprised how quickly and easily people list the basic characteristics of worship, nurture, service and outreach that make up church life.

   You now have a list of those things which will make up the final statement and an indication of what the church considers most important.

3. The same small group drafts an initial statement – or perhaps each member of the group makes a draft or selects or adapts one of the initial sentences which seems representative of the whole.

   You now have a draft, or drafts, of your mission statement.

4. The church council, or another meeting of the whole church, approves or selects (and probably

amends) the statement. There will be some important preliminary questions: Has anything been missed out? Is the language as striking and as memorable as possible? Does everyone feel happy with the process so far and included in it?

You now have your mission statement.

All this could happen over a few weeks. Straight-away you need to put the statement to work. It provides the criteria for your planning and decision-making. It articulates the vision of the church you feel God calls you to *be*. It starts to inform you of what you are now called to *do*. It would be also good to review what your church is actually doing in the light of how the statement describes your purpose.

EXAMPLE

St Mary's, Hightown produced a mission statement. They were surprised how easy it was and how much agreement there was about the purpose of the church. The statement read:

> St Mary's exists to give Jesus Christ a face in Hightown through the quality of its worship, its fellowship and its mission.
>
> St Mary's looks to encourage its members, and the people of the community of which it is a part, to realise their full potential as children of God.

When they started to use the statement to plan ahead it was easy to identify three clear priorities: worship, nurture and outreach. They were able to relate these to their credal understanding of the church. Worship was about being a holy church.

Nurture was about being a catholic church. Outreach was about being an apostolic church.

When they analysed their life in the light of the statement they quickly became aware that very little happened in their church to give Jesus a face through their fellowship with one another. Apart from some occasional social events, Lent groups and the Mothers' Union, there was not much else happening. As for mission, there was nothing other than the occasional offices and a good relationship with the local school. Of their three primary areas of purpose – worship, fellowship and mission – only worship really took a priority in what actually went on, and even this could hardly be said to give Jesus Christ a face.

This striking phrase, which had come out of one of the first sentences put down by a member of the church, seemed to stand in judgement on much of their church life: could the face of Jesus be seen in their church? The second clause of their statement was equally challenging. It was about the quality of their Christian life. Was it about keeping the show on the road or bringing people to their full potential in Christ?

When they looked at the agendas of their church meetings they were struck by how much time was spent discussing the day-to-day issues of maintenance. Although these remained vitally important they set themselves a new set of priorities: to renew their worship so that Jesus could be seen in it; to develop fellowship and nurture in the church; and to discover how to do evangelism. This was perhaps the hardest admission of all: that they did not know where to begin with evangelism. They thought it was something evangelicals did, and on the whole they felt rather uncomfortable about it. It conjured up images of painful encounters, knocking on the doors of strangers, or embarrassing rallies where people were exhorted to give their lives to Jesus.

They set about a painful task of liturgical renewal, and in particular there was renewed teaching about the sacraments as encounters with Jesus. Although this had a dramatic effect on the worship, much of it took place in the area of fellowship. They adopted a cell structure for their church in which every member of the church was put in a fellowship group which met once a month. Even though only about half the congregation actually attended, everyone knew they were part of a group and the groups happily took on basic responsibilities for pastoral care as well as providing a forum for fellowship, prayer, Bible study and Christian teaching. They also began to explore models for evangelism which would resonate with their theology and spirituality.

The mission statement spurred them into life. For the first time in a long while they felt as if they were all marching to the same tune. This did not mean that there were no disagreements. If anything there were more. The difference was that there were some agreed criteria whereby disputes could be judged. Whereas in the past disagreements had been factional, now they were tactical. It was about how they put their vision into action, rather than arguing about the different outcomes of different visions. Best of all it was discovered that people who had major disagreements with the way the church was going found themselves wrestling with God rather than the Vicar!

They saw their mission statement as a tool. Everyone in the church was given a copy, and a short planning document was produced which showed how the different elements in the statement were beginning to be shaped into a parish plan. But the vision was not static. They did not pin their statement on the wall and admire it. They put it to work in the exciting business of becoming a missionary church. Producing their mission statement helped them realise the more fundamental truth: that God was calling *them* to be his mission statement.

Within a few years they had forgotten about the statement and in another few years they would probably have to agree another one – even if, as is likely, they came up with the same few basic things, but worded differently. The point is that it belonged to them: it was their self-understanding under God of what it meant to be the church. For the first time in a long while they felt they were going somewhere.

The New Evangelism

From Damascus to Emmaus

The phrase the *new evangelism* was first coined, I believe, by John Finney. He describes a paradigm shift in the way we think about evangelism. The controlling biblical paradigm for coming to faith is less likely to be Paul's encounter on the road to Damascus than Cleopas and his companion's encounter on the road to Emmaus.[7] This does not come as a great surprise to Catholic Christians: we readily talk about the journey of faith. However, John Finney's research at the beginning of the Decade of Evangelism has clearly demonstrated that coming to faith *gradually* is in fact the experience of the vast majority of Christians.[8]

We could say that we used to think evangelism looked like this:

CONTACT

COMMITMENT/
CHURCH MEMBERSHIP

According to this view, evangelism was a fairly straightforward process. There were a lot of people 'out there' in the world who were not Christians, and the task of evangelism was to make contact with them and bring them to commitment to Christ and membership of the church. In fact, as we have already begun to see, the changed nature of the culture in which we evangelise, and the actual experience of those who are coming to faith, make it hard to believe that evangelism could ever be adequately depicted by a straight line. When we make contact with people today we cannot assume they have any knowledge of the Christian faith and the traditions of the Church. They will probably be deeply suspicious of any universal claims to truth that we might make, and will be ill at ease with the concepts of sin, forgiveness and salvation with which we might try to describe the Christian story and claim its relevance to their life.

Turning seekers into travellers . . .
In other words, if we were to depict evangelism diagrammatically we would probably want to draw a long and meandering line. There would be many false starts, cul-de-sacs, wrong turnings and back-tracking. While it remains true that some people will have the sudden conversion that a straight line depicts, most people will want to place something else between contact and commitment. I would call this something *nurture*.

This is what evangelism actually looks like:

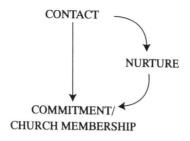

CONTACT

NURTURE

COMMITMENT/
CHURCH MEMBERSHIP

... and travellers into pilgrims ...

Between contact and commitment a journey takes place. People who start out by simply asking questions of life, seeking after a deeper truth and a greater sense of value and purpose, become fellow travellers with the church, involved in a process of nurture where they can ask their questions and experience something of the true nature of Christian life. In time these travellers become pilgrims. Faith is awakened in such a way that the things they had longed for in life – security, peace, self-worth, value etc. – are recognised at their heavenly source rather than in their many earthly manifestations. We will say much more about this and about a Catholic understanding of conversion and salvation in the second half of the book. For the moment it is important to see how the tasks of evangelism are closely related to the process of the journey, and how a journey of discovery looking for meaning in life becomes a holy pilgrimage where we discover not just satisfying answers, but God himself. But first of all we need to be in contact with people in our communities. Secondly, we need to find ways of helping them make the journey. Thirdly we need to bring them to commitment. The straight line is still there – people who come to faith suddenly – but the emphasis is on the accompanied journey of the curved line.

The phrase 'accompanied journey' comes from the language of the catechumenate. This is probably the key evangelistic strategy for the church today. It has its roots in the life of the early church, where initiation was properly understood as a long-term process. Nor was it just about church membership: the aim was active discipleship. Therefore the diagram needs a further dynamic:

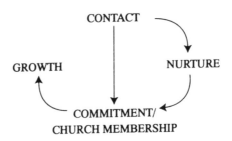

... and pilgrims into apostles

The evangelistic process does not stop when people become members of the local church. It overflows into what I am calling *growth*. This is a massive issue for the Church today. Many members of our congregations are faithful Christians, in so far as they attend church regularly, but have not grown into that maturity of faith whereby they feel able to live the Christian life Monday to Saturday. Christian faith has never become much more than an important, but nevertheless secondary, adjunct to a basically unchanged life. Church becomes something you do, when it should be something you are. Growth is stunted.

Evangelism must, therefore, never be satisfied with anything less than the making of disciples which is Christ's commission. This goes way beyond the standard six to ten week confirmation course which is still the basic model of initiation in too many churches. We must aim for a changed life.[9]

The effect of this changed life is the living of the Christian life in the world. Our diagram can be completed in this way:

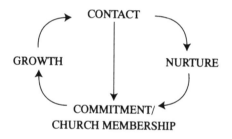

I call this the growth spiral. The fruit of seeing the process of evangelism as the making of active disciples is more contact. This is the best sort of evangelism: the Christlike witness of ordinary Christians in their everyday lives.

It is when we try to short-circuit the circle and go only for the straight line evangelism that it becomes the counter-productive and often artificial task that gives the gospel a bad name. When discipleship is seen as the goal of evangelism, witness, service and proclamation flow together in a life properly focused on Christ and on the building of his Kingdom. Evangelism just happens. It happens not because it has been dragged in artificially, but because it is the most natural consequence of a Christian life. We cannot help but put into action the saving truth which now shapes our life. We cannot help but speak of the things we have seen and heard.[10]

So much of this is linked to prayer. Growth in discipleship is not growth in knowledge *about* God, but growth in relationship *with* God. It is not information but transformation.

The catechumenate

The terms I have used in this diagram – contact, nurture and growth – are the same as in the programme for evangelism and discipleship that I had a part in producing, *Emmaus: the Way of Faith*. This programme sets out to make the thinking of the catechumenate more accessible for the Church today across a spectrum of churchmanship and denominational traditions. While of itself it is not doing anything original – as we have already noted the catechumenate is in the DNA of the Church – it is startling how little the thinking of the catechumenate has passed into the consciousness of the Church, especially among Catholics, with whom it would seem to find its most natural home. Even the ubiquitous Alpha course, which does understand the evangelistic task as a process, does not go beyond a ten-session course of basic instruction. It was interesting to see that the Roman Catholic bishops of England and

Wales in commending Alpha described it as 'pre-evangelism'. What Alpha provides is a raw encounter with the gospel. It is excellent that this is seen to happen over a period of time and within the context of a community where questions can be asked and relationships develop, but it is still a couple of steps removed from the more thoroughgoing journey of faith of the early catechumenates. Some of these took three years, and while we may balk at the idea of running confirmation classes that last such a period of time, we must aim for something more thorough: something which has the potential to equip people for Christian living in the world. To this end it is my belief that we must begin to shape the life of our churches around the task of initiation. After all the pattern of our Church year – Lent the final period of preparation before baptism at Easter – is derived from the process of evangelism and nurture which shaped the early church. *Emmaus* is one resource on offer which clearly links initiation and discipleship with evangelism.

Evangelistic aims for the missionary church
The Emmaus programme also provides us with some realistic aims for evangelism as we seek to accompany people on a journey into faith. The first concerns making contact with people and helping them begin the journey: *it is about turning seekers into travellers.* The second concerns the process of nurture and how we help bring people to commitment: *it is about turning fellow travellers into pilgrims.* The third is about commitment flowing into discipleship: *it is about turning pilgrims into apostles.*

This is how these categories of spiritual growth relate to our diagram:

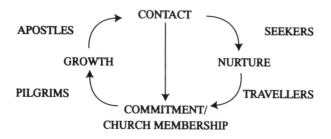

The second half of this book will show how this can work in the life of the local church. We will travel round this growth diagram showing how people can be accompanied from a position of interested unbelief to committed and active discipleship.

Step 2 – Understanding how evangelism works
As we have already noted, many people are scared stiff of evangelism. It is associated in people's minds with coercion, manipulation, triumphalism, dogmatism and plain embarrassment. Even though the reality of how evangelism actually happens in the vast majority of churches is a million miles away from these fears, many churches still do not have evangelism on the agenda. Even those churches which have a mission statement and a mission strategy often let evangelism sit on the back burner. Phrases like 'well, everything is evangelistic' and 'we are called to be evangelists' allow the church to avoid doing anything specific.

First, we need to teach the church, and especially those in lay leadership, how evangelism works for most people. Study of John Finney's book, *Finding Faith Today*, will be invaluable here. The diagram that has been presented in this chapter, and the aims which flow from it, also need to be presented and understood.

One of the best ways of doing this is to ask your PCC or your congregation to reflect on the story of their own faith. You can conduct your own piece of research. Get people to tell each other how they came to faith and then ask them to put themselves into categories, working out who had dramatic Damascus Road type experiences – there will be some – and who had gradual Emmaus Road type experiences – this will be the vast majority. Using the categories in John Finney's book, you might also like to work out what were the main and the contributing factors that helped people come to faith. Was it through the occasional offices? A life crisis? An activity of the church? A family member? A friend?[11]

Once people realise that there is a new way of understanding evangelism, it is relatively easy to start developing the structures and ministries in the church that can enable progress to be made.

It is also immensely valuable for Christian people to reflect on the story of their own faith. Another key insight of the Decade of Evangelism has been a shift away from seeing evangelism as the communication of doctrinal truth to the sharing of a spirituality as a way of life. It is not insignificant that the primary documents of the Christian Church are *stories* of faith. Christian people in the day to day task of evangelism should be sharing two beautiful and unique stories: the story of what God has done in Jesus Christ and the story of what God has done in their own life.

At St Mary's their mission statement clearly identified evangelism as part of their missionary task. They wanted members of their community to find their full potential as children of God. But they did not really know how to make this happen.

At a PCC meeting every member was encouraged to share with their neighbour their own story of faith. When these stories were analysed it turned out that of the eighteen people present only one had had a dramatic conversion experience. All the others told stories of gradually coming to faith. With some they only realised they had become a Christian when they looked back. Many had come to church since infancy. For them it was important to share the story of when their faith became real, or the story of how they had lapsed and returned to faith. For about half the PCC it was the first time they had ever told anyone about their own faith story.

From this exercise it was easy to demonstrate the basic truths of the new evangelism:

1. *Coming to faith is more like a journey than an event.* Nearly everyone told a story of gradually coming to faith. When the diagram of contact/nurture/commitment/church membership and growth was shown people were readily able to remember these different phases of their own spiritual growth.

2. *The best sort of evangelism is the Christlike witness of ordinary Christians.* The key factors leading to faith nearly always involved family members or close friends.

3. *Belonging comes before believing.* Everyone spoke of the importance of being welcomed into the life of the Church; of fellowship; of a church that was able to accompany people on the journey from interested unbelief to committed faith.

As a church they now could see several priorities for the way they were being called to work: evangelism must become a continual dimension in the whole life of the church, not just an occasional activity; the church was not supposed to have a mission, it was supposed to *be a mission.* This would mean placing an even higher priority on deepening the faith of those who already came to church so that they could grow into an apostolic faith. It would also mean setting up structures for nurture and looking creatively at how they could use the contacts they already had. It would also mean making new contacts. As they explored this approach to evangelism it became clear that most of the PCC knew very few people outside the church. The business of running the church had voraciously consumed most of their time and energy, so that contacts with non-Christians were almost non-existent. Not only did they realise how important it was to develop in themselves a sense of their own responsibility for carrying forward God's mission, they also saw the need to streamline church structures. Room needed to be made for new initiatives in the areas of contact and nurture. Space needed to be found so that committed church people could develop friendships and relationships outside of church life. As they began to do this so they also began to build the structures that would enable people to discover faith.

PART TWO
SEEING PEOPLE COME TO FAITH

Seekers into Travellers

Making contact

The term 'seekers' is a good one for describing how many people feel today. They will not particularly like this description, and it is probably best to avoid it in any mission publicity, but nevertheless many people in our society are feeling dissatisfied with the ideas and institutions that shaped their lives and which promised so much. There is a feeling that there must be more to life. No doubt the Church itself is seen by many as another outmoded and redundant institution, and we do see a continuing decline and loss of confidence in the institutional life of the Church. But the gospel is different. While people may not be attracted to the institutional life of the Church, the person of Jesus and the promise of the Kingdom still appeal with radical clarity. As Catholic Christians we need to have a very high doctrine of the Church as the pilgrim people of God – people who are on the way – but a very low doctrine of our particular structures and institutions. These may well collapse around us, but the demise of this *way* of being church does not mean the demise of the Church, and certainly not the demise of the gospel. Yet for many priests their vision for being a Church centred on service to the world is tarnished by the ever-increasing demands of keeping the institution up and running. Well, as we have already noted, there is little choice but to do both. We must maintain the Church as we have inherited it, and we must also look to build the Church of the future. It is in making contact with those outside the Church who are seeking after some way of making sense of life, and in nurturing them into the faith, that these issues will begin to resolve themselves. It is in giving that we receive. By focusing outside ourselves on the needs of our community, and on the people we are called to serve, we shall discover what it means to be a missionary church.

Using contacts

Every church is in contact with thousands of people. The question is: how do we use these contacts creatively? Take a standard funeral visit. Many priests find that the bereaved person is asking questions of the nature of life and death, the very questions that begin a journey to faith were there enough time to visit the person regularly. But it is not possible to do more than one visit because there is another funeral tomorrow, and two more next week, and two the week after that. It is hard enough to visit before and after each of these funerals, let alone make a whole string of visits. Consequently, the person is prayed for, offered to God and forgotten about in the busyness of parish life. People are invited to come to church, but they rarely show up. Even when they do, one is painfully aware of how difficult it is for them to make sense of the liturgy, arriving cold for the first time and with hardly any previous contact with the Church. The journey to faith ends before it has started.

Having a lay ministry team for visiting obviously makes an enormous difference, but there are still severe limitations on how much time can be given to one-to-one visiting of this kind. In terms of the spiritual life, if the person does not progress fairly quickly towards a point where they feel quite motivated to join the church, the opportunity is lost. One cannot establish the sort of one-to-one relationship that would really make the difference, so it is come to church or nothing. Although Catholics make a lot of the evangelistic opportunities of the occasional offices (and we can all point to the one or two successes of these encounters), in practice the 'come to church' of this kind of pastoral evangelism is little different from the 'come and be saved' of a more campaigning style. In both cases there is little to offer the person who needs to make a gradual journey.

Where churches have established a place of nurture there is the possibility of these pastoral contacts being transformed. Instead of the choice being between a long series of visits, which will be impossible for most churches to maintain, or an invitation to come to church on Sunday, there is an opportunity to join a group of people, Christians and other seekers, exploring what faith is about.

This place of nurture can take many different forms. The most obvious, and probably the most fruitful, is some sort of enquirers' group. Here, people can explore the claims of the Christian faith and, because the best of these groups will be made up of Christians and seekers, can experience something of the Christian life. As we have already noted, one of the key features of the new evangelism is that belonging comes before believing. Those who are seeking need to feel comfortable: they need to feel that their questions and concerns are taken seriously.

Beginning a journey

Becoming a Christian is not just learning things about the Christian faith, it is about becoming a member of the Christian community, and it is about relationship with a God who is himself a community of persons. Therefore, right at the beginning of the journey, people need to experience what it means to be part of a pilgrim Church. Before these people can become pilgrims themselves they need to feel happy to travel with us and be open to experiencing life from a Christian perspective.

The term 'travellers' describes those people who are on the way. They may not yet be coming to church, but they are committed to taking the next step – going through a course of enquiry or attending special events that the church is organising.

Creating contacts

Initially, the most important thing for a church to do is to create a place of nurture. This makes it possible to use our existing contacts creatively and help people begin the journey. For too long evangelism has been disproportionately concerned with making lots of new contacts. Unless we have the structures to help bring people to faith, and then establish them in the life of faith, this will not only consume all our energy, it may well prove fruitless. As we are beginning to see, initial contact and a first proclamation of the gospel, be it in words or deeds, cannot be separated from an evangelistic process. But this does not mean that we should never think about making contact with those outside our immediate circle of contacts. It is a matter of priorities.

Having established a place of nurture, here are some ideas for creating contacts. These ideas for basic evangelism need to be built into the ongoing life of the church. They should not be seen as 'one-offs'; as a church develops an evangelistic heart, it will also develop a programme of contact events which, in time, will feed into the nurture process.

I. DOOR-TO-DOOR VISITING – THE BÊTE NOIRE OF EVANGELISM

Some parishes take a few streets each month and deliver, by hand, a copy of their parish magazine. Others audit the parish by knocking on every door, or a sample of houses, asking what people feel about local issues and how the church might help. In both of these cases the church is operating in servant mode. The emphasis is on how the church can help, rather than what the church wants. One of the most effective of these ways of visiting is prayer visiting. Here the church knocks on doors in the neighbourhood and asks if there is anything, or anybody, the residents would like prayed for. Usually people doing this kind of visiting are astonished by the positive response they receive.

2. EVANGELISTIC EVENTS

These can be very effective provided real thought is given to who will come and what kind of event they might come to. Unless you have a very big name indeed (and how many of these are there in the Christian world?) and very professional publicity, people will not 'just turn up'. They will come because a friend from church has invited them, and, usually, brought them as well. It is no use, therefore, having a really good speaker at a service in church if ninety-five per cent of the congregation would not dream of bringing their friend to a church service. The best events are often on neutral territory – a pub, a school hall etc. – and have a strong social element – a dance, a quiz, a meal. This does not mean that there can be no specifically Christian content, but people need to know what they are coming to. If there is going to be a speaker you need to say so; but sometimes it will be enough just to introduce people to the *idea* of the church. A good social event can put the church back on the map and show that the Christian gospel connects with life. These things are much better demonstrated by deeds of service and celebration than pious words.

3. SERVICE TO THE COMMUNITY

There are many ways that this could happen, and there is lots of overlap with what a church is probably already doing. The chief thing is to listen to your community. What are its needs? Where can the church help? This attitude of attentive service then overflows into all sorts of projects which in turn provide all sorts of evangelistic opportunities – parent and toddler groups; lunch clubs for the elderly; services in sheltered housing or old people's homes; after-school clubs etc.

Developing leadership
When the church begins to operate in this way, further issues about the shift from seeker to traveller also arise. The place of nurture that will be right for one group of people – say, residents in a sheltered housing block – will not necessarily be right for another – say, young parents. Often, the place of nurture arises out of the place of contact. It is very important to be flexible. The pattern of nurture that a church decides upon must be adaptable so that it can cross-fertilise into different situations. This will also require lay leadership. Once the place of nurture is established it is vitally important to begin training lay leaders. This is not as difficult as is often imagined. The biblical model for training is apprenticeship. This is what we need in our churches. Too often we send lay people off on lengthy training courses, whereas Jesus said 'follow me' – and you will learn on the job! If, at the beginning, the priest is the only person in the church ready and willing to lead a nurture course for enquirers, then from day one it will be very important to have the deputy, apprentice leader in place. By going through the whole of the course once, and slowly sharing some of the responsibilities of leadership, this person will be ready not only to lead a group, but to apprentice another leader. This is the model we need to foster in our churches, and I have seen it work in some of the most deprived parishes of urban Britain.

To build missionary structures into the ongoing life of our church development of lay leadership is absolutely vital.

Step 3 – Building the place of nurture
This will be some sort of nurture course where those who are seeking will become fellow travellers learning about the ways of Christian faith, but not yet actual pilgrims committed to Christ and his Church. There are several good resources providing materials to run such a course and they are listed, and briefly evaluated, at the end of this chapter.

In the early part of a church's journey towards becoming a missionary church it will probably not be possible to run a course like this more than once a year. This is because of limits of time, leadership and, most crucially, people to come on the course! However, it is important to be proactive. Put the dates in the diary for the course before you have any candidates. Not only does this speak clearly of the new priority mission is taking in the life of the church, it will have the psychological effect of helping everyone in the church gear their thinking towards outreach. Once the course is advertised all the pastoral work that is already happening can now be focused towards recruiting a group of people to begin this process of discovery. Some churches run a series of one-off events during the year, usually on neutral territory like a pub, and then invite people to their nurture course.

In time more courses can be run each year, but another reason why many churches could only run one course a year is that this is not the end of the journey. We hope to see travellers become pilgrims. For some this will happen during the nurture course. This must always be our hope and churches working this way are always surprised and delighted by the massive development people who seemed so far from the gospel can make even in a fifteen-week course. For others it will happen later. Others will fall away.

Although some sort of nurture course is vital for helping people make the journey of faith, we need always to remember that God is the Evangelist. In the next chapter we shall look in more detail at what it actually means to become a Christian and see the different ways that people make the crucial step of faith, and how we can best facilitate this as fellow companions on the road.

EXAMPLE

St Mary's decided to run an Emmaus nurture course once a year. They put the dates in the diary in the early summer, planning for it to begin on the week following Advent Sunday. This wasn't a great time for newcomers – the build-up to Christmas – but they liked the idea of a fresh start at the beginning of the Church's year. This also gave them enough time to begin inviting people to come, and the hope that one or two might say yes. Everyone felt very apprehensive. There was a lot of disagreement about whether anyone would come; about whether they should spend more time deepening their own faith before they tried to share it with others; about who would lead the groups; about where they should take place. Eventually they decided that they could spend forever waiting to be ready and it was much better just to begin. The first course would be led by their priest with two apprentice leaders. The groups would meet in the home of one of the lay leaders and, if the numbers grew, in the church hall (not ideal, but there was nowhere else in the parish). Anyway, they did not think large numbers would be their problem. They were fearful that no one would come and, for this reason if no other, they decided each person who came as an enquirer would be given a sponsor. They had read about the role of a sponsor and liked the idea of someone having a ministry of companionship towards the person who was seeking. Best of all they thought it would help make a viable group if only one or two signed up.

In September and October they had two outreach events to help encourage some of the contacts they already had to make the next step. They held a men's breakfast in the church hall. Twelve church people brought between them seven non-church friends. They had a fry-up, a five-minute talk about the Christian faith from their priest, and a short testimony from one of their own laymen. He had never done anything like this before and was eaten up with nerves. He only spoke for a few minutes, but it was astonishingly powerful. He just said how faith had made a difference to his life. He spoke about the loneliness of suffering and of two occasions in his life when he had felt very alone: when his brother had died from cancer, and when he had lost his job. He said how he had known the presence of God in his suffering, and how he had felt solace in loneliness. He said he felt stupid saying all this: because men didn't usually talk about their feelings. But he also said that God was real for him.

After the breakfast people were told about the nurture course that was starting in the autumn. One person signed up a couple of weeks later. Everyone said they had had a good time and another event for the men of the church was planned for the future.

The other outreach event was a walk for families on a Sunday with a picnic. This was supposed to emphasise the idea of faith as pilgrimage. In the event it rained and everything had to happen indoors in the church hall. The walk metamorphosed into an impromptu activity day. Everyone had terrific fun. It was gathered together in a short act of worship in church. The priest spoke about the children's activities in church on Sundays, and his plans for an after-school club. Four non-church families came along. Nobody signed up for the nurture course, but two years later, when the after-school club got started, two of these families became Christians and the parents went through subsequent nurture courses.

The first course began with nine people: four enquirers; two sponsors (each sponsoring two people); and three leaders – the priest and two apprentices. The four enquirers were a man from the breakfast, a widow from a funeral visit, and a couple who had been on the fringes of church life for years and came just because they were invited.

The course ran for fifteen sessions in three blocks. At the end of each block it was possible to drop out and in the event this was exactly what the couple did at the end of the second block. But the other two went on to finish the course and at the end of the second block were welcomed into the life of the Church. Both of them had reached a point where they wanted to become Christians and join the Church. It was funny for them coming to church for the first time, but because of the fellowship they enjoyed in the group there were people they knew who would look out for them and help them understand the liturgy. They used the rite of welcome from Emmaus to show that these two fellow travellers wished to become pilgrims, to be confirmed, and to enter the life of the Church. They were confirmed in Eastertide and the following autumn (this time pre-Advent) when the second nurture course was run both of these new Christians invited friends of theirs to come on the course. The second course had eight enquirers, five of whom went on to be baptised or confirmed. There were also now two or three people in the church who were able to lead courses. They were hoping to run one in the community centre in the parish where a monthly service for the elderly had produced a number of people who had lapsed from faith and wanted a refresher course, and also a few new people wanting to explore the idea of confirmation. Also the after-school club was running and this had created a whole network of contacts with young parents. This might also mean running a small course during the day. But they were ready for this. It was possible to imagine running two or three nurture courses each year. They were adapting the material so it really fitted their parish. They were also running follow-up groups so that those who had become Christians were not left in the lurch once they had been brought to initial commitment. Something was happening in their church. Two years after beginning the nurture course, and three years after they had first begun their missionary journey, they were conscious that for the first time in twenty or thirty years the size of their congregation had grown. But even more exciting was the raising of the spiritual temperature. They were discovering for themselves that spiritual and numerical growth go hand in hand.

Resources

1. *ALPHA*

This is the famous ten-session nurture course from Holy Trinity, Brompton. It is widely used by a huge number of churches and is very effective. In particular it places the sharing of the gospel within a social context: every *Alpha* meeting is supposed to begin with a meal. The teaching method is quite up-front – a talk or video followed by smaller discussion groups. It will not, therefore, transfer so well into small group situations where the whole thing needs to be home-based and discussion-based. Its main weaknesses from a Catholic perspective are not so much what it says but what it doesn't say. *Alpha* comes from a Charismatic Evangelical background and therefore does not cover some aspects of faith that some Christians would consider basic. There is, for instance, hardly anything about the sacraments. But having said this, quite a few Catholic parishes, both Roman and Anglican, use *Alpha*.

Alpha is published by Kingsway.

2. THE CATECHUMENATE NETWORK

This is a group within the Church of England which

seeks to encourage and facilitate catechumenate thinking. They have published a starter pack for parishes which, although not professionally produced, is still very good for churches which would favour a more exploratory approach to nurture than the more prescriptive methods of *Alpha* and *Credo*.

Their starter pack is available from:

The Catechumenate Network,
Tithings New Barn,
Swalcliffe,
Banbury,
Oxon OX15 1DR

3. *CREDO*

This is the Church Union course written and presented by Bishop Lindsay Urwin. It follows a similar approach to *Alpha* but the content gives a much broader sweep of the gospel story and has much greater emphasis on church and sacrament. There is a video with talks by the Bishop, and again the emphasis is on input rather than exploration.

Credo is published by the Church Union.

4. *EMMAUS*

This is based on a catechumenate model but still has a fifteen-session nurture course at its heart. This course tries to strike a balance between explanation and exploration. It is less prescriptive than *Alpha* or *Credo* but not as open-ended as the Catechumenate Network approach. There is liturgical material – rites to mark the different stages of the journey – and information about sponsors to accompany people on the journey. Emmaus has three stages – Contact,

Nurture and Growth – and is published in six volumes, so, unlike the other materials, starts a lot earlier and goes a lot deeper. Whatever course is used, the Emmaus Contact book will be of enormous benefit in thinking how you will get people to come on a course, as will the Emmaus Growth modules for following up basic instruction and exploration. The authors of *Emmaus* come from a cross-section of Christian traditions.

Emmaus is published by the Bible Society and National Society/Church House Publishing.

5. *FOLLOW ME*
This is a Confirmation Pack from the Additional Curates' Society, with a strong Catholic emphasis, widely used by Catholic parishes, but now looking rather dated in terms of design, if not of content. It also follows a catechumenate model: twenty sessions with liturgical material and advice about sponsors. There is material for adults, teenagers and children.

Follow Me is published by the Additional Curates' Society.

6. *GOD FOR GROWN UPS*
This is a varied book of material from the Roman Catholic Church, originating in the diocese of Nottingham. The introductory material is particularly good.

God for Grown Ups is published by Redemptorist Publications.

Travellers into Pilgrims

Conversion

It is not always possible to identify the moment along the way when a fellow traveller becomes a pilgrim. Some people do have dramatic conversion experiences and are completely turned around; others encounter a series of signposts which steadily change their direction; others find that it is only in looking back that they can see the new route that has been taken. Whatever the individual experience, the term pilgrim describes well the new orientation of life. All of us experience life as a journey, but without God, however rich and meaningful life is, it is going nowhere. Death is the final destination and then nothing. Faith changes life in all sorts of ways, but most dramatically the journey of life now becomes a journey home. We find the centre of our life is no longer located within ourselves, or in what we see around us, but in God. We let go of the things of this world and cleave to the things of heaven. But far from losing our joy in the world around us, in our relationships and our passions, it is given back to us tenfold. By putting Christ at the centre of our lives we discover the radical gospel truth that he has put us at the centre of his. To be a pilgrim, then, is to be in right relationship with God and in right relationship with the world. Our life has a destination and a purpose, but, because we also know God as the source of all life, we are given an abundant joy in the journey.

This is focused in the incarnation – God's total identi-fication with all that he has made – and in the ascension – God's taking of his creation to himself. To know that you are a pilgrim is the first stage of Christian discipleship. It gives a new direction to life.

Repentance

But a new direction implies there was an old one. Even though we live in a society which has largely stopped believing in sin, people will be aware that life is changing. The more a person glimpses the new direction of life that the Christian faith offers, the more they will be aware of the failures and short-comings of what went before. Life will no longer be lived for self alone, it will be focused on God.

Love of self for self's sake is the beginning of all sin. It is the denial of our interdependence with one another and with the creation: it is the denial that we are children of God, made for relationship with him.

Some Christians say that we should tell people the bad news first – speak of the reality of sin and the damage it does – before telling people the good news of salvation in Christ. I do not take this view, and I do not think it is the Catholic way. Our motiv-ation for evangelism is not to save lost souls from hell (we must leave issues of final judgement to God alone) but to share the good news of the fullness of life that we have found in Christ. We remind people that they belong to one another and that they belong to God.

Many people in our society today suffer enough from low self-esteem and lack of self-worth without receiving a further battering from the Church. But neither should we duck the issue of sin. After all, the gospel is about forgiveness.

As people begin to discover the reality of Christian faith on the journey of nurture, so there will come a point where it is natural and appropriate to speak of repentance. Its literal meaning is 'turn around'. It is the conscious reorientation of life: it is when someone begins to see their life as a pilgrimage, and not just a journey. Michael Marshall puts this well: repentance is not seeing a different world 'so much as the same world differently'.[12]

Commitment

The rites of baptism, Confirmation, or a renewal of baptism, clearly contain prayers of repentance and reorientation – I turn to Christ; I repent of my sins; I reject evil. However, many new Christians will have particular issues that they will want to deal with. This can be done through prayer and through counselling, especially a ministry of listening, but for most new Christians it will be very important to make a confession. The sacrament of reconciliation is given for the purpose of helping people appropriate the full impact of the gospel. Reconciliation *is* the gospel. God is in Christ reconciling the world to himself. In Christ God acts decisively to bring us into union with him. He comes to look for us. The cross is therefore the ultimate meeting point between humanity and God. It is a place of ignominy – the scandalous death of an innocent man reveals our capacity for inhumanity. It is a place of triumph – the self-giving love of Jesus reveals the loving heart of God. Baptism is our sharing in this triumph: it reveals the new direction of life as well as wiping away the harmful effects of the old one. The sacrament of reconciliation is a personal way of receiving and re-appropriating this gospel truth.

It is powerful good news for people to hear the words of absolution being spoken to them personally, and to be set free from the sin which had stifled their spirit and which they had so often sought to suppress (this is what we do with sin in an age which pretends everything is relative).

A personal response of this kind is often the crucial step to becoming a disciple of Jesus. We need to understand not just the abundant grace of the sacrament, but the psychological significance of being able to make a definite and personal step forward. As people proceed on a nurture course and discover faith dawning within them, or for that matter if faith comes suddenly, the final stages of preparation for initiation need to include a definite invitation to take seriously the gospel call to repentance. The sacrament of reconciliation is the best way to do this, but sometimes it will be important to spend time with people individually and to help them make a prayer of personal commitment.

All this is of prime importance to the evangelistic process. It helps establish people in the faith. It is also important to note that this is an issue which is all too easily ducked. Many clergy have had little experience of seeing adults come to faith. We, therefore, sometimes shy away from encouraging a definite response.

Becoming a Christian is a response of our whole being to the love of God. Decisively, this includes the will: we decide to follow Christ and to try to live our lives by all that that entails. Faith may dawn slowly, but a decision to become a Christian must have its reality in an actual turning-point. The journey always reaches a point where there is a decision: shall I go on? Can I take all that this path holds? (It is in this sense that we say baptism is the beginning of the journey, not the end.) The important point is that if this does not happen in the dramatic circumstances of a conversion experience (and it probably won't for most people) then baptism or Confirmation provides an actual point of decision. This needs to be prepared for, and particular thought needs to be given to the inclusion of prayers of repentance. The sacrament of reconciliation provides a way of making a personal step of faith to mirror the public step of initiation.[13]

Step 4 – The step of faith
The inner journey of the heart – the process of nurture where people gradually move from seeking to travelling to pilgrimage – reaches its turning-point in the rites of initiation. Publicly these are baptism, Confirmation and Eucharist, but there is also the personal response that is often best provided for through the sacrament of reconciliation. All those who are involved in the initiation process, especially the clergy, need to be conscious of the different dynamics of the heart and the will. These come together in the decision to follow Christ. But they require different handling. On the one hand we need to be prepared to go the second mile, conscious that people's development into faith rarely matches the timetables of our nurture courses; and we also need to be ready to challenge for a response, helping people to make the

decision that is clearly emerging into view. This is as much about apologetics as it is about evangelism. Quite often people are prevented from making the step of faith because there are barriers in the way. We need to be ready and able to deal with these, even if it will often be the case that we have no conclusive answers. Being prepared to listen is always the first prerogative. We need to remember that Jesus is Emmanuel – the God with us in the midst of difficulty and suffering – as well as the God who saves.

By tenderly caring for those who are coming to faith and by boldly challenging for response we will see people make the step of faith.

EXAMPLE

The two people who came to faith on the first nurture course at St Mary's were confirmed on the Second Sunday of Easter. One of them was also baptised. Their sponsors and a large group from the congregation accompanied them to the church on the other side of the diocese where the service took place. It was very moving.

On the day before the Confirmation they had both made their confession and the one who was being baptised did not receive absolution then, so that the baptism itself – entry into the sacramental life as well as the beginning of the Christian life – could be the moment of forgiveness. Neither of them particularly wanted to make a confession but it was explained to them as a chance to make a personal response to God in preparation for the public response of the Confirmation. It was like a spring-clean, making room for God and making space for his Spirit to dwell. By this time neither of them needed convincing of the reality of sin: the more they learned of Jesus the more they realised that their biggest failings were not what they had done, but what they had failed to do. It was a big step actually to share this with someone else. But after they had made their confession they were filled with a great joy. Not only had it been good to let go of some of the baggage from the past, it was a wonderful feeling to know that they were loved and accepted. A few days after the Confirmation someone at work, commenting on this new-found faith, said to one of them that the Church was full of hypocrites. Yes, she replied, and there is always room for one more! The truth that the church is a band of pilgrims, repentant sinners taking the cure, was really beginning to take hold in their lives and in the life of the whole church. The moment of confirmation by the Bishop seemed like a turning-point – a real confirmation of all that had already happened, and a new beginning for life. The knowledge that they were children of God that had awakened within them, was now matched by a bold determination to live as citizens of heaven.

Pilgrims into Apostles

Discipleship
Commitment to Jesus and membership of the Church is not the end of the story, it is just the beginning. As Bishop Michael Marshall has noted, the aim of evangelism is not to drag the world into the church, but to pour a spirit-filled church into the world. Our aim is not more church members, but active disciples. We therefore need to do a thorough job of initiation. Whatever happened in the nurture stage needs to be built upon so that those who now know their life to be a pilgrimage are also conscious of the apostolic call: like the first disciples they too are being commissioned to live and share the gospel.

Growth
For many churches the problem is not so much getting people as keeping them. If all the people who had joined the church over the last twenty years had stayed, our situation today would be remarkably transformed. There are many reasons why people lapse away, but chief among them is our failure to take the ongoing process of initiation seriously, especially in the first couple of years of a new Christian's life.

These are the main issues that need to be addressed.

I. BELONGING

Being a Christian means being a member of a community of faith. All the time we need to be nurturing and developing our fellowship in Christ. Opportunities to share faith together, socialise and pray are vital for church growth.

Belonging is also about feeling cared for. As a church grows in number it becomes much harder to maintain a system of pastoral care where the priest feels able to know and regularly visit every member of the congregation. This model of pastoral care creates a growth ceiling which is unlikely to see a congregation grow much beyond 100–150 people. A growing church needs a new model for pastoral care. Regular groups – cells of the church – provide a place where people can feel that they are known and cared for. The lay leaders of these groups are vitally important people and the priest will find a lot of his time will be spent in their ongoing support. It will probably also be necessary to create a lay visiting team so that the work of pastoral care is shared by the church. Basic pastoral care has to become *one another* care.

But this issue goes beyond care to affect the quality of church life. We have not spoken much about the Sunday morning life of the church – there is just not space in a book of this size – but, undoubtedly, if your church is growing it will be because the worship on Sunday is energising and attractive. This is just as important as having proper structures for evangelism, nurture and growth. It is a sad fact of church life that as the number of people coming to church increases, the quality of church life decreases. The church feels less intimate, more impersonal etc.

A cellular structure for church life creates a place where people feel they belong and where they are cared for: it is the context in which growth in other areas can take place.

2. THEOLOGY

We need a theologically literate church. While we are quite good at equipping one or two of the keener members of the congregation to go and undertake some sort of theological study, the vast majority of our people have only a very slender grasp on the intellectual credibility of the Christian faith. The Scriptures say that we should all be able to give a reason for the hope that is within us.[14] It is in the local church that people should be learning about their faith and exploring its relevance for life. We cannot live the apostolic life unless we are able to speak about our faith both as personal testimony – what it has meant for our life – and as saving truth – what it means for every human life and for the whole of creation.

This is a massive task, and it is an area of massive failure. I believe that the key to becoming an evangelistic church is this equipping of the people of God to be able to speak about their faith personally and convincingly.

3. SPIRITUALITY

We need an apostolic spirituality for an apostolic life: an 'as you go' spirituality. Robert Warren defines spirituality as 'how we encounter God and how that encounter is sustained'.[15] At the heart of a renewed Catholic spirituality will be the Eucharist. Here God is encountered in his Word, in his people and in the sacrament itself. Eucharistic theology also enshrines the gospel paradox that things need to be broken open before they can be shared. It is with broken bread that we share the body of Christ.

We need to be a people who regularly break open the Word of God. This needs to happen in our liturgy, in our groups and in our homes. The Scriptures need a greater place of honour in Catholic spirituality.

We need to be a people who are ourselves broken open in love to one another and in service to the world. It is these acts of sacrificial love that will, more than anything, begin to convey the radical truth of the gospel. It is in service to one another that we shall sustain our encounter with Jesus.

We need to be a people who drink deeply from the sacramental well. The sacraments are given to the Church as channels of grace. There needs to be more teaching in our churches about the evangelical power of the sacraments, especially the Eucharist, reconciliation and healing. The world cries out for value and meaning, for forgiveness and for healing. These are the very things entrusted to us in the sacramental life. We can receive from Jesus the new value of being citizens of heaven; we can feed at his table; we can hear his words of absolution; we can be assured of the ultimate promise that all will be well, and in the midst of terrible suffering we can discover his passion and death, and that the God who made the world, not only loves it, but has entered it. He is the God who seeks out every human heart and who comes to listen, to serve and to love.

In these ways we will, in our own day, carry the marks of the apostolic Church which we identified in the first chapter – a lively and credible faith, resonating with the culture of the day and testified by holy lives.

Step 5 – Ongoing growth

A missionary church needs structures to maintain the growth of new Christians and preserve the intimacy and fellowship of a growing church. If we do not do this we will lose people out of the back door just as fast as we welcome them in at the front.

The chief elements in this are:

1. Ongoing groups for growth
2. Shared pastoral care
3. Shared leadership

This will be particularly hard on the priest who will have to move from being the person who provides the primary care for the church, to being the one who ensures primary care is provided.[16] This is a new role, but no less priestly. The priest needs to become the servant of a servant church encouraging the priesthood of the whole people of God.

I think this will also mean a greater emphasis on the sacramental life of the church and on encouraging an apostolic spirituality. The church will become much more a house of prayer and a centre for teaching, service to the community and celebration. It will be in smaller groups, and in people's homes, that people will learn to pray together, to break open the Word of God and to practise the mutual love and service which is the heart of a gospel life. I would hope that the home would become a centre for liturgical life as we rediscover our Jewish heritage and experience being church as a daily reality, not just a Sunday duty.

EXAMPLE

In the very first phase of becoming a missionary church St Mary's had adopted a cell structure and encouraged everybody in their congregation to attend one meeting a month for ongoing growth. The two new Christians who had been through the nurture course joined the group that their sponsors went to. This became the place where they could grow in their understanding of the faith and in fellowship. It was also the place where they could begin to think about the apostolic life and discover that they too had a responsibility to share the gospel with others.

As the church grew larger over the next few years new cells had to be created, and sometimes a group doing the nurture course could naturally become a new cell for growth. Tensions arose in the church. The priest found he was no longer able to remember easily the name of everyone in the congregation; the intimacy and warmth that had so characterised their worship when there were sixty people in the congregation were noticeably lacking when there were over a hundred. It felt really good to be in a growing church, but it was not without its problems, and he was beginning to feel more and more stressed. The answer lay in developing new structures for pastoral care. The cells took on more responsibility to look out for one another, and those who were not in cells

– about half the congregation – were visited by a lay visiting team. The expectations of this 'one another care' were basic (making sure everyone in the church was visited by another member two or three times a year and making sure that everyone was contacted if they missed more than the odd Sunday) but it made a huge difference, not least to the priest. He felt his role was changing, but as he was able to let go of some front-line pastoral responsibilities, so he was able to devote more time to developing lay leadership in other areas, and to using his own particular gifts to the full. Slowly the church developed structures where growth could be sustained. The services on Sunday were becoming large celebrations with a strong family emphasis, owing to the large numbers of children now attending through the after-school club, but the cell groups and a varied pattern of other worship were providing for the other needs of spiritual growth and a sense of belonging. As the spiritual temperature slowly rose so it was evident in people's lives. Morale was higher than it had ever been, and this overflowed in service to the community and in evangelism.

For so many years St Mary's had totally over-estimated what it could achieve in the short term, and totally underestimated what it could achieve in the long term. Ten years after their journey to become a missionary church had begun, one of the first people to become a Christian started a small 'Agnostics Anonymous' discussion group during lunchtime at work. When asked why she was doing this she quoted Peter who, when warned to stop telling people about Jesus replied, 'We cannot stop speaking about what we have seen and heard.'[17]

Questions

Becoming a Missionary Church
1. Does your church have a mission statement?

2. If so, what are you already doing which needs affirming? What is not working and needs amending? What is missing and needs introducing?

The New Evangelism
1. How did you become a Christian? Share this story with someone in your church.

2. What thrills you most about being a Christian? Share this with somebody.

Nurture and Evangelism
1. Does your church have a place of nurture?

2. Who are you in contact with outside the church? Write down their names under the headings 'friends', 'relatives', 'neighbours' and 'colleagues'. How can you pray for these people? Serve them? Witness to them?

Travellers into Pilgrims
1. What is repentance?

2. What is conversion?

Pilgrims into Apostles
1. How are people in your church enabled to grow in their faith?

2. What evidence is there for the gospel in your life?

Notes and References

1. Donald Elliott, paper written for the Council of Churches for Britain and Ireland Conference for World Mission quoted in Robert Warren, *Signs of Life* (Church House Publishing, 1996), p. 90.
2. John 10:10.
3. Matthew 28:18–20.
4. John 17:21.
5. 'Snow' from *Collected Poems* (Faber, 1966).
6. See Lindsay Urwin, 'Of Maypoles and other dances', in *Church Observer*, Winter 1996 (published by the Church Union), pp. 3–6.
7. John Finney, *Recovering the Past, Celtic and Roman Mission* (Darton, Longman and Todd, 1996), p. 40. It is important not to make too much of the distinction between the Emmaus and the Damascus roads. It is a useful shorthand for the way thinking about evangelism is developing, but Paul's dramatic experience on the way to Damascus can clearly be seen in the context of a more gradual journey, just as Cleopas and his companion's gradual experience on the way to Emmaus contains its dramatic experience as Jesus is suddenly made known in the breaking of bread.
8. The detailed research of *Finding Faith Today* (Bible Society, 1992) showed that about 70 per cent of people coming to faith experienced this as a gradual process. Of the 30 per cent who described a sudden conversion many of these saw it in the context of a longer process.
9. Robert Warren, the National Officer for Evangelism in the Church of England, has argued for seven ways in which our lives should be transformed through the process of initiation: spirituality; self-acceptance; changed character; community; worldview; lifestyle and mission. These can be followed up in Cottrell, Croft, Finney, Lawson and Warren, *Emmaus: the Way*

of Faith, Introduction (Church House Publishing and the Bible Society, 1996), pp. 18–24.

10. See Acts 4:20.

11. Factors leading to faith are listed on p. 36 of *Finding Faith Today*.

12. Michael Marshall, 'The double grip of glory' in Jeffrey John (ed.), *Living Evangelism* (DLT, 1996), p. 17.

13. For those who are preparing for baptism a confession can be made and the baptism itself can serve as the absolution.

14. 1 Peter 3:15.

15. Robert Warren, 'Renewing the Church around Spirituality' in *Good News*, Issue 26, March 1997, p. 7.

16. I am indebted here to Steve Croft for his thinking about the relationship between evangelism and pastoral care, a much neglected area in church growth theory.

17. Acts 4:20.

Further Reading

Becoming a Missionary Church

Cottrell, Stephen, *Sacrament, Wholeness and Evangelism* (Grove Books, 1996)

Warren, Robert, *Being Human, Being Church* (Marshall Pickering, 1995)

    Building Missionary Congregations (Church House Publishing, 1995)

New Approaches to Evangelism

Abraham, William, *The Logic of Evangelism* (Hodder & Stoughton, 1989)

Clarke, John, *Evangelism that Really Works* (SPCK, 1995)

Cottrell, Croft, Finney, Lawson and Warren, *Emmaus: the Way of Faith, Introduction* (Church House Publishing/Bible Society, 1996)

Finney, John, *Finding Faith Today* (Bible Society, 1992)

    Recovering the Past: Celtic and Roman Mission (Darton, Longman and Todd, 1996)

Haring, Bernard, *Evangelisation Today* (St Paul Publications, 1974)

Warren, Robert, *Signs of Life: How Goes the Decade of Evangelism?* (Church House Publishing, 1996)

Nurture and Evangelism

Ball, Peter, *Adult Believing* (Mowbray, 1988)

Croft, Steve, *Growing New Christians* (CPAS/Marshall Pickering, 1993)

Dodd, Christine, *Making RCIA Work* (Geoffrey Chapman, 1993)

Grundy, Malcolm, *Evangelisation through the Adult Catechumenate* (Grove Books, 1991)

The Nature of the Christian Faith

Doctrine Commission of the Church of England, The, *The Mystery of Salvation, The Story of God's Gift* (Church House Publishing, 1995)

John, Jeffrey, *This is Our Faith* (Redemptorist Publications, 1995)

Young, John, *Know Your Faith in a Decade of Evangelism* (Hodder and Stoughton, 1991)

Growth and Discipleship

Croft, Steve, *Making New Disciples* (Marshall Pickering, 1994)

John, Jeffrey (ed.), *Living Evangelism: Affirming Catholicism and Sharing the Faith* (Darton, Longman and Todd, 1996)